NATIVE AMERICAN NATIONS

THE SHAWNEE

BY LIZ SONNEBORN

CONSULTANT: TIM TOPPER, CHEYENNE RIVER SIOUX

BLASTOFF! DISCOVERY

BELLWETHER MEDIA • MINNEAPOLIS, MN

Author's Statement of Positionality:
I am a white woman of German, Danish, Swedish, and Swiss descent. As such, I can claim no direct lived experience of being a Native American. In writing this book, however, I have tried to be an ally by relying on sources by Native American writers and authors whenever possible and have worked to let their voices guide its content.

This edition first published in 2024 by Bellwether Media, Inc.

No part of this publication may be reproduced in whole or in part without written permission of the publisher.
For information regarding permission, write to Bellwether Media, Inc.,
Attention: Permissions Department,
6012 Blue Circle Drive, Minnetonka, MN 55343.

Library of Congress Cataloging-in-Publication Data

Names: Sonneborn, Liz, author.
Title: The Shawnee / by Liz Sonneborn.
Description: Minneapolis, MN : Bellwether Media, 2024. | Series: Blastoff! discovery: Native American nations | Includes bibliographical references and index. | Audience: Ages 7-13 | Audience: Grades 4-6 | Summary: "Engaging images accompany information about the Shawnee. The combination of high-interest subject matter and narrative text is intended for students in grades 3 through 8"– Provided by publisher.
Identifiers: LCCN 2023023104 (print) | LCCN 2023023105 (ebook) | ISBN 9798886874440 (library binding) | ISBN 9798886876321 (ebook)
Subjects: LCSH: Shawnee Indians–Juvenile literature.
Classification: LCC E99.S35 S66 2024 (print) | LCC E99.S35 (ebook) | DDC 305.897/317–dc23/eng/20230606
LC record available at https://lccn.loc.gov/2023023104
LC ebook record available at https://lccn.loc.gov/2023023105

Text copyright © 2024 by Bellwether Media, Inc. BLASTOFF! DISCOVERY and associated logos are trademarks and/or registered trademarks of Bellwether Media, Inc.

Editor: Rebecca Sabelko   Series Designer: Andrea Schneider
Book Designer: Laura Sowers

Printed in the United States of America, North Mankato, MN.

TABLE OF CONTENTS

HOME IN THE OHIO VALLEY	4
TRADITIONAL SHAWNEE LIFE	6
EUROPEAN CONTACT	12
LIFE TODAY	16
CONTINUING TRADITIONS	20
FIGHT TODAY, BRIGHT TOMORROW	24
TIMELINE	28
GLOSSARY	30
TO LEARN MORE	31
INDEX	32

HOME IN THE OHIO VALLEY

The Shawnees make up a large Native American nation from the eastern United States. Their original land is in the middle Ohio Valley. This area includes parts of what are now Ohio, Indiana, Kentucky, West Virginia, Pennsylvania, and other eastern states.

The Shawnees speak an **Algonquian** language. *Shawnee* means "southerners." Related nations living to their north might have given them this name. Other Algonquian-speaking nations closely related to the Shawnees include the Kickapoo, the Fox, and the Sac.

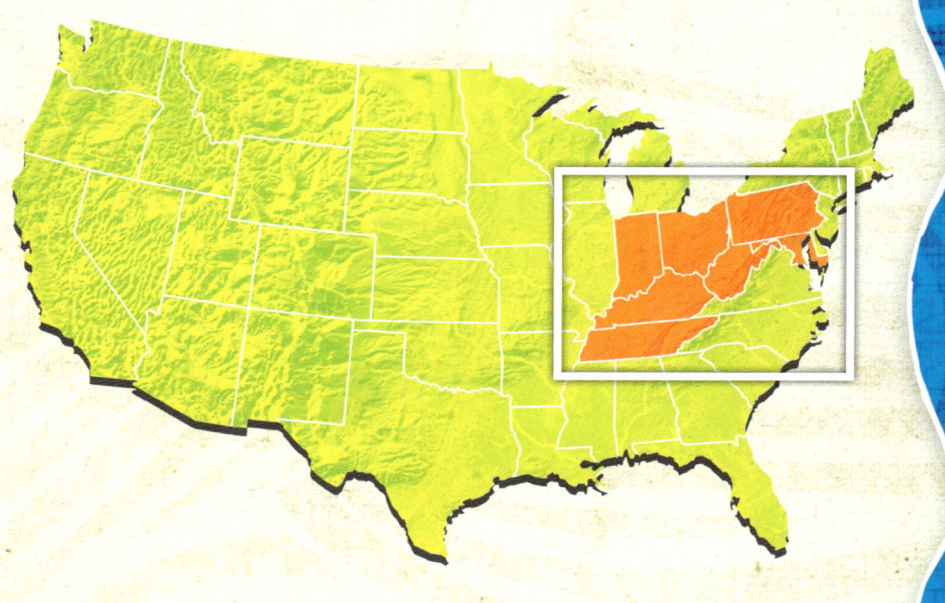

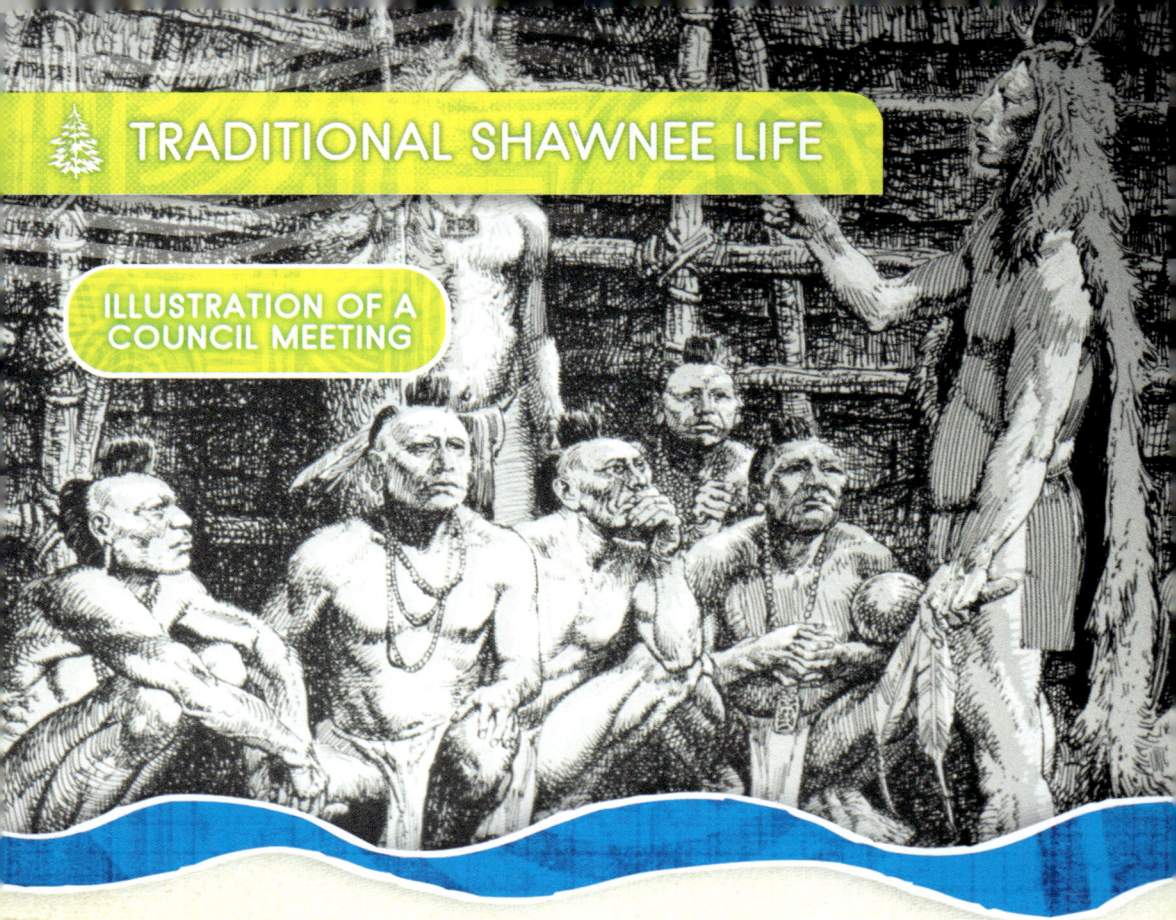

TRADITIONAL SHAWNEE LIFE

ILLUSTRATION OF A COUNCIL MEETING

The **ancestors** of the Shawnee tribe had five **divisions** that were led by the Principal Chief. Each division had a different role. The Mekoches, for example, handled business with other Native American communities. The largest Shawnee villages were likely tied to a division. Each of these villages had two leaders. The Peace Chief oversaw **ceremonies**. The War Chief led warriors into battle.

Early Shawnees lived most of the year in villages. Families lived in wigwams for part of the year. These houses were made of pole frames covered with tree bark or animal skins. Each village had a **council** house made of logs. A tribal council of Chiefs and elderly men met there.

LEADING THE SHAWNEES

Most Shawnee Chiefs were men. But sometimes women related to male leaders could become village Chiefs.

SHAWNEE RESOURCES

POLE FRAME

CORDS

COVERINGS

WIGWAM

ILLUSTRATION OF A SHAWNEE VILLAGE

The Shawnees' ancestors relied on farming, hunting, and gathering for food. Fields surrounded each village. Women planted corn, squash, and beans. They gathered roots and fruits. They also tapped maple trees to make syrup.

SHAWNEE HUNTERS

Some early Shawnees left their villages for hunting camps during the winter. Men spent days hunting deer, squirrels, rabbits, and turkeys. They used clubs and bows and arrows to kill their prey. They made clothing and shoes from animal skins and furs.

Religious ceremonies are important to the Shawnee way of life, and some Shawnees carry out the ceremonies today. They believe these ceremonies bring good harvests and protect their people. The Shawnees believe that the goddess Kokumthena gave these ceremonies to the people. Her name means "Our Grandmother."

Kokumthena gave bundles of **sacred** objects to each Shawnee division. These bundles are very powerful. By properly caring for the bundles, the Shawnees are protected from harm.

SPIRIT HELPERS

Traditionally, older Shawnee children were sent alone into the woods to find a spirit helper. The Shawnees believed spirit helpers protected them throughout their lives.

EUROPEAN CONTACT

ILLUSTRATION OF AN ATTACK ON A EUROPEAN SETTLEMENT

Shawnee life was changing by the 1600s. The Shawnees were greatly affected by European **settlers**. Many died from battle or from illnesses brought from Europe. The European fur trade caused fighting over hunting grounds between the Shawnees and Haudenosaunee. The Haudenosaunee had pushed the Shawnees from the Ohio Valley by the mid-1600s. The Shawnees broke into smaller communities. They spread out in all directions.

Many Shawnees had returned to the Ohio Valley by the mid-1700s. But settlers wanted control of the land. In 1763, the Shawnees joined other Native American communities in **Pontiac's Rebellion**. The Shawnees were forced to give up much of their land.

ILLUSTRATION OF OTTAWA CHIEF PONTIAC IN 1763

In 1795, the Shawnees were forced to give up even more land. Shawnee leader Tecumseh united different Native American communities. They tried to stop settlers from taking over their lands. But they were unsuccessful.

The U.S. government's many forced **treaties** divided the Shawnees into different communities during the 1800s. Some Shawnees moved to the Mexico **Territory** before 1825. Later becoming the Absentee Shawnee, they were forced into Oklahoma Indian Territory after 1848. Today's Eastern Shawnee Tribe moved to Oklahoma in 1831. In 1869, today's Shawnee Tribe were forced onto the Cherokee **reservation** in Oklahoma.

FAMOUS SHAWNEE

TECUMSEH

BIRTHDAY 1768

DEATH 1813

FAMOUS FOR
United Native American communities to try to stop settlers from taking their lands

ILLUSTRATION OF THE TREATY OF GREENVILLE, 1795

WHY "ABSENTEE"?

The Absentee Shawnees got their name from an 1854 treaty. It noted that they were "absent" from the treaty talks.

LIFE TODAY

Today, the Shawnee nation is made up of members of the three Shawnee tribes of Oklahoma. Some Shawnees live and work on tribal lands. But many live throughout the U.S. and the world. They work in schools and hospitals. They run businesses. Some work to carry on their **traditional** practices.

Each of the Shawnee tribal governments is in Oklahoma. The Absentee Shawnee Tribe is near Shawnee, Oklahoma. There are more than 4,600 members. The Eastern Shawnee Tribal government is in Wyandotte, Oklahoma. The Tribe has around 3,500 members. The Shawnee Tribe has over 4,000 members. Its government is in Miami, Oklahoma.

ABSENTEE SHAWNEE GOVERNMENT BUILDING

THE LOYAL SHAWNEES

The U.S. government used to refer to the Shawnee Tribe as the Loyal Shawnees. The tribe was loyal to the U.S. government during the American Civil War from 1861 to 1865.

Each Shawnee tribal government works for its members. The Shawnee Tribe has a Tribal Council led by the Chief. The council runs elections. The Business Council makes laws and business decisions. The Absentee Shawnee Tribe is led by a Governor. The Eastern Shawnee Tribe is led by a Chief. It has a Business Committee that leads business decisions and tribal committees. It also makes laws.

Each tribe provides programs such as health and education. The Shawnee Tribe and the Eastern Shawnee Tribe also run businesses. The Shawnee Tribe runs a casino with the Chickasaw Nation. The Eastern Shawnees run two casinos.

GOVERNMENT OF THE SHAWNEE TRIBE

SHAWNEE TRIBE

TRIBAL COUNCIL
- Chief
- Second Chief

BUSINESS COUNCIL
- Seven council seats

SHAWNEE TRIBAL COURT

BEN BARNES, CHIEF OF THE SHAWNEE TRIBE

THE ABSENTEE SHAWNEE FLAG

The great military leader Tecumseh appears on the Absentee Shawnee Tribe's flag. The flag also features the phrase *Li Si Wi Nwi*, which means "among the Shawnee."

CONTINUING TRADITIONS

WAR DANCE

Some Shawnees practice their traditional religion. The Absentee Shawnees hold celebrations at their tribal ceremonial grounds. Each May, the spring Bread Dance celebrates planting crops. A War Dance in summer celebrates the first crops of the year. The fall Bread Dance in October honors the harvest.

The Eastern Shawnee Tribe hosts a **Pow Wow** each year in Wyandotte, Oklahoma. Members wear traditional clothing. They compete in dancing and hand drum contests. The festival also includes traditional storytelling and foods.

POW WOW IN WYANDOTTE, OKLAHOMA

SHAWNEE LANGUAGE APP

The Eastern Shawnee's government has a department dedicated to keeping the tribe's **culture**. It hosts gatherings and events. The tribe also developed a language **app**. The Shawnee Tribe Cultural Center shares stories and traditions of the past through tours. Guests can see cultural items and art and attend events. The center also has a mobile museum!

The government of the Absentee Shawnees hosts classes. They teach members how to make traditional yarn belts, ribbon skirts, and more.

TRADITIONAL SHAWNEE INSTRUMENTS

WATER DRUM

GOURD RATTLE

FIGHT TODAY, BRIGHT TOMORROW

All Shawnees are in danger of losing the Shawnee language. Shawnee is still spoken by some Absentee Shawnees. But very few members of the Eastern Shawnee Tribe or Shawnee Tribe know the language.

SCHOOL WHERE PRESCHOOLERS LEARN THE SHAWNEE LANGUAGE

The Shawnee Tribe is looking to change that. In 2020, the government started a free language program. It started with Shawnee language classes in three Oklahoma communities. The program has grown to include a language learning website. It allows Shawnee people to learn the Shawnee language no matter where they live.

The U.S. government is trying to find out more about government-run **Indian boarding schools**. The Shawnee Tribe also wants the U.S. government to look into schools that were not run by the government. In the mid and late 1800s, many Shawnee children were sent to these schools. Like in government-run schools, Shawnee children were taken from their parents. They were punished if they practiced their culture. This is one reason why so few Shawnees speak their native language today.

INDIAN BOARDING SCHOOL IN KANSAS

The Shawnees' efforts to preserve their culture show their strength. Their fight has helped them survive over many centuries. It will allow them to keep their traditions alive into the future!

TIMELINE

1774
Led by Chief Cornstalk, Shawnees in present-day Kentucky battle invading settlers but the Shawnees are forced to give up their land

STARTING IN 1640
The Haudenosaunee Confederacy begin the Beaver Wars that result in the Shawnees being forced out of the Ohio Valley by the end of the 1600s

EARLY 1800s
Shawnee leader Tecumseh tries to unite Native American peoples to keep settlers from taking over their lands

1795
Shawnee leaders are forced to sign the Treaty of Greenville and give up land in present-day Ohio

1763 TO 1765
The Shawnees join other tribes in Pontiac's Rebellion to fight Europeans who were settling on their land

1936
The Absentee Shawnee Tribe of Indians of Oklahoma is founded

2018
The Shawnee Tribe Cultural Center opens in Miami, Oklahoma

1936
The Eastern Shawnee Tribe of Oklahoma is founded

2000
The U.S. government recognizes the Shawnee Tribe as an independent Indian nation

GLOSSARY

Algonquian—related to a family of languages spoken by Native American peoples throughout areas of North America

ancestors—relatives who lived long ago

app—a program such as a game or internet browser; an app is also called an application.

ceremonies—sets of actions performed in a particular way, often as part of religious worship

council—a group of people who meet to run a government

culture—the beliefs, arts, and ways of life in a place or society

divisions—groups

Indian boarding schools—schools created throughout the 1800s to remove traditional Native American ways of life and replace them with American culture

Pontiac's Rebellion—an armed conflict between united communities of Native Americans, led by Ottawa Chief Pontiac, and the British Empire from 1763 to 1765

Pow Wow—a Native American gathering that usually includes dancing

reservation—land set aside by the U.S. government for the forced removal of a Native American community from their original land

sacred—relating to religion

settlers—people who move to live in a new region

territory—an area of land under the control of a government; territories in the United States are considered part of the country but do not have power in the government.

traditional—related to customs, ideas, or beliefs handed down from one generation to the next

treaties—official agreements between two groups

TO LEARN MORE

AT THE LIBRARY

Bodden, Valerie. *Shawnee*. Mankato, Minn.: Creative Education, 2020.

Jones, Kadeem. *Shawnee*. New York, N.Y.: PowerKids Press, 2016.

LaPlante, Walter. *Tecumseh*. New York, N.Y.: Gareth Stevens Publishing, 2016.

ON THE WEB

Factsurfer.com gives you a safe, fun way to find more information.

1. Go to www.factsurfer.com.

2. Enter "the Shawnee" into the search box and click 🔍.

3. Select your book cover to see a list of related content.

INDEX

Absentee Shawnee Tribe, 14, 15, 16, 17, 18, 19, 20, 23, 24
app, 22
ceremonies, 6, 10, 20
Chiefs, 6, 7, 13, 18, 19
culture, 22, 26, 27
divisions, 6, 10
Eastern Shawnee Tribe, 14, 16, 18, 21, 22, 24
future, 27
government of the Shawnee Tribe, 18
Haudenosaunee, 12
history, 6, 7, 8, 9, 10, 11, 12, 13, 14, 15, 17, 25, 26
homeland, 4, 5, 12, 13, 14
housing, 6, 7
Indian boarding schools, 26
Kokumthena, 10
language, 4, 22, 24, 25, 26
map, 4, 5, 16
members, 16, 18, 21, 23, 24
name, 4, 10, 15, 17
Ohio Valley, 4, 5, 12, 13
Oklahoma, 14, 16, 21, 25
Pontiac's Rebellion, 13
religion, 10, 20
settlers, 12, 13, 14
Shawnee resources, 7
Shawnee Tribe, 14, 16, 17, 18, 19, 22, 24, 25, 26
Shawnee Tribe Cultural Center, 22
spirit helpers, 11
Tecumseh, 14, 19
timeline, 28–29
traditional Shawnee instruments, 23
traditions, 6, 7, 8, 9, 10, 11, 16, 20, 21, 22, 23, 27
treaties, 14, 15
tribal council, 6, 18
tribal government, 16, 17, 18, 22, 23, 25
U.S. government, 14, 17, 26

The images in this book are reproduced through the courtesy of: Mikael Males, front cover, pp. 20, 21, 23 (gourd rattle); Tloventures, p. 3; Kenneth Keifer, pp. 4-5; Angel Wynn, pp. 6, 8-9, 10-11, 23 (water drum); IllustratedHistory/ Alamy, p. 7 (leading the Shawnee); ST-art, p. 7 (pole frame); Fburnette, p. 7 (cords); Norm Lane, p. 7 (coverings); Gary Whitton/ Alamy, p. 7 (wigwam); New York : Strohmeyer & Wyman/ Library of Congress, p. 9; Science History Images/ Alamy, p. 12; Alfred Bobbett/ Wikipedia, p. 13; Library of Congress/ Wikipedia, p. 14; G1816/ Wikipedia, p. 15; kennethaw88/ Wikipedia, pp. 16-17, 24-25; Xasartha/ Wikipedia, pp. 18, 19 (Absentee Shawnee flag), 29 (Absentee Shawnee flag, Eastern Shawnee flag); SOPA Images/ Getty Images, p. 19; wichayada suwanachun, p. 22; Associated Press/ AP Images, pp. 26, 27; JF233/ Wikipedia, p. 28 (1774); Dana60Cummins/ Wikipedia, p. 28 (1795); Gerry Bishop, p. 31.